PRAISE FOR THE WORK

In a long poem composed of lyric fragments, Necessary shows us how pieces of a world coalesce and drift or are sundered apart. The poem's vast range of reference gives this writing a sense of continuous, restless movement: the reader navigates time and site as the poem wrestles with itself "to question an account/traverse a distance." Though David Harrison Horton is a writer of some restraint, Necessary nonetheless rings with urgency. It is by turns outraged, weary, yearning,— in short, always ready "to feel the complications/to feel." At a most vexed and painful time in human history, this is indeed necessary writing: it enters the fray to truly, bravely "reckon a human position."

— *Elizabeth Robinson, American poet,*
professor, and author

You will find a world in David Harrison Horton's Necessary that you neither understand, nor see yourself in, nor know what to do with, and you will read to the end all the same. In this calm, lonely account, east Asia and North America are completely different and more or less the same, Biblical prophets and the Elizabethans do much the same work, the non sequiturs and disappointments of classic Chinese poetry (think Tao Yuangming or Liu Tsung-Yuan) are what the pool game Marco Polo was preparing us for. Or as Necessary puts it: "the books Mr. Lusk bought / the ones he intends to read". If you look closely, or if you read quickly, out of the corner of your eye, you will see the curious silhouette of an honest person. As the poet writes, "All right, but you have to promise not to cry."

— *Jordan Davis, American poet and former poetry editor of The Nation*

David Horton's Necessary — its sharply chiseled nine-lines-per-page "sketches" arranged, apparently randomly, into 1-, 2-, 3- . . . 9-line "units" whose Cubistic shifts of attention from present tense concrete detail ("slippers and sandals / hammer-toed children / one pair of pants between"; "repetition of the factory floor/ sound of steel-toed shoes") to thoughts moving through the mind ("The purpose of sketches / hagiography"; "a time not to speak of / a time"; "historical society placard / monument to the dead / votives and progression // proverbial historical"; "to be in a state too long / to be in a state") -- is indeed necessary reading for anyone who wants to know what's really going on in China these days.

— *Stephen Ratcliffe, American poet, critic, and author*

Necessary

ALSO BY DAVID HARRISON HORTON

Model Answers
(CCCP Chapbooks/subpress, 2024)

Maze Poems
(Arteidolia, 2022)

Necessary

DAVID HARRISON HORTON

First published July 2025 by Downingfield Poetry, an imprint of Downingfield Press Proprietary Limited, Suite 346 / 585 Little Collins Street, Melbourne Victoria 3000, Australia. For a full list of addresses and contact information, visit www.global.downingfield.com

Text copyright © 2025 David Harrison Horton. Typesetting and book design copyright © 2025 Downingfield Press Proprietary Limited. All rights reserved.

Without limiting the rights under copyright reserved above, in accordance with the Copyright Act 1968 (Commonwealth of Australia) no part of this publication may be reproduced, stored in or introduced into a retrieval system, or transmitted, in any form or by any means (electronic, mechanical, xerographic, recording, or otherwise), without the prior written permission of the copyright owner and the publisher of this book, except for brief passages quoted for the purpose of criticism or review.

David Harrison Horton asserts their right to be known as the author of this work.

ISBN 978-1-9235130-0-6 (paperback)
ISBN 978-1-9235130-2-0 (e-book)

Book and cover design by M. Cheng-Mader. Cover image used under licence.

Downingfield Press undertakes its work on the traditional lands of the Wurundjeri people of the Kulin Nation and pays respect to Elders past, present, and emerging.

DOWNINGFIELD PRESS PROPRIETARY LIMITED
MELBOURNE · LONDON AND MONTRÉAL

 A catalogue record for this work is available from the National Library of Australia

In the necessary light

ebb and faltering among shadows
shapes and false imagery

a soldier's helmet
rifle

a faked empathy
fakement

big ball entwined

—Let the dirty fuckers eat dirt

What it means in these parts
collected

marrow from the jaw strap
elbow

a brood and murder wire
tracked to the heart

—Git ye gone, Joan
sleeved and sorrowed

the village hermaphrodite

How the crow moves
ostensible winter

shingled and slated

dinner plate well plated
all along the Clinton

how her hair sets
cold as windshield
chill of chilled glass

story of someone's mother

Cut cord and stanchion
measured by palms, pony

acreage and miles
view of the settlement

tractor cuts and hectares
orchard

everything one could want
less

the need for less

Companionless and weary
anthologized

the heart a weak remembrance

the way the clay sticks to the shoe
impeded reading

the way the scent becries a scenery
tossed in among
scuttled
evening greys on blacks

Expanse the heritage

the measurement of fences
milk cows

how the Saracens traversed the desert

night voices and wind
the only good road

what to do with wives
obstinate cattle

how well the fire burns for the dead

Table scraps
the linens
the women who take care of such fare
the banter between

how she sings when she is not happy
boredom's barometer
how she smiles

fall and fallow
simultaneously

That Cathay is treacherous
under unjust rule

that the peregrines be well-kept
as the season of buck and hare

migratory populace
suburb behind every wall

money double stamped and accepted
good for wares along the route

whores outside the city

Largish palmetto
lathe boards and wiring

how squalor gets re-amended
defined

how the crippled earn their keep

how the enjambment is faulty

how every town in Michigan
claims Edison worked their station
boxed ears and all

How there is evidence
Mr. Lusk in Chicago
mackintosh

how third person prose excludes the reader

how the train stop was quaint
unimpressive

scarlet beetle on a bamboo stalk
scarved women of the *hutong*

how he did please

To count friends on fingers
scrimshawed bone
requirement

I am afraid the call cannot be placed
to place

—Marco
—Polo

—Marco

—Marco?

Calculation of mercy
Hosea
desert sand is the same

Cornish hen on largish plate
rectory

what is meant and said
Ts. Campion
scuttle secondary

advice

Mr. Godston in Chicago
contemporaneous

five acts one day
Racine

the one hand and the other utter strangers
a bottom deck deal

—Did we pay the toll twice?

to reckon distance
the loneliest highway

The need for a steady check
mythology
Mr. Maupin's attire
cauliflower

she had pursed lips

Christ, how the head hurts
to contemplate
bucket full of brine

bystander

Winged it good but not dead
a limit

that sheep and dogs maintain

issue of vocabulary

the worst sound you ever heard
the worst sight

how dogwoods pay reverence without calendar
and death needn't know our names
familiar enough with the circumstances

The marsh and valleys
recurrence

the accent the hometown gave you
the one you acquired

the suit you wore the first day of work
how you pissed away the check

to be only no. 4 killer
to botch the job entire

to envision snow before it falls

To account for
to share a burden
to revise a statement

to look into the eyes of others

to reckon a good friend dead
to reckon

to gaze blank faced upon a peasant field
bad crop and all

to blink

After the cross
nothing is lost

how nobility survives poverty

if no one hits it
how can it fall?

there are men enough to face the darkness
living and dreaming alone

there are men enough
merry-go-rounded, lost

A dead kingdom
telephone service
expiation

how to walk through the woods

—The only road I could have taken
was the one I took

Diderot's nephew
Lei Feng

how they all dance so well together

Akiba's mistake
a narrow-walled city
paper and iron tigers
an enemy

reckoned figures
parchment

yindao

shale
no appeals to horizon

To crow a city
skyline

reversal

the women of Shouting Hill
a *kang*
a thorn

a time not to speak of
a time

a time

How to measure a thought
to mince words
to become beyond reproach

slippers and sandals
hammer-toed children
one pair of pants between

unlike a reservoir
unlike the Christ

unlike the whole goddam thing

To accrue wealth
girth and bridge

take the card with both hands
sit back to exit

tax codes, tariffs
execution

Mr. Lusk felt it a sham
burial eyes

felt

André's sad attempt
the speech that killed it
the dance of aftermath

in this light I cannot tell
in this light nothing is clear
in this light I just do not know

I do not know

the Fathers have been silent
quiet as mittens

How a country is born
a past rectified

how the shit one shovels gets accepted

neither word nor plainsong
every other thing a form

to wash one's face in the ocean
egg dish on Shouting Hill

faithless Virgil a sorry guide

the use of dogs to track a dead scent

The most common radicals
conference on borders
where to find the nearest train

to be in a state too long
to be in a state

ceramic tiles
shops along the *hutong*
night stands

burden

Her virginal heart
seated in Majesty
chapterhouse

how the devoted flock
factor the accounting

how the stone grows cold
and wine turns

dance card punched
even bet in the third

A few paternal acres bound
a rabbit box
collapsible shed

plum showers
the month of June

to beat the proverbial brick
cord of winter oak

in everything confidence
to never skimp a vice

To reach a fatal shore
aped the plan entire
sucked the wolf's tits dry
map of the subway

how the shirt hangs on her shoulders
Montana

to do a bit of wandering
lingered the sky double stationary
to pick olives off the tree

Lattice work and dry
to shuffle the waters
coxcomb and said
Mr. Lusk Pencil Factory stature

to have waited out a hope
to have waited

saint of migrant fools
James of dumpster placement
his most beatified hands

The way the good worry
what she feels within

bamboo with few leaves

diced upon the counter
ripcord and sail

corrugated gift horse
Westphalia

to consider concerns

to run with a broken shoe

A balcony dialogue
a steer

Mr. King is thinning in Oakland
fakement I has lost his humor
Mars sits mute towards the hill

mortgage and sentiment cannot assist
a maddox in place of a shovel

bodiless profile and song
the works entire

To reach a point
to reach

Valerie beatific

coarse lined walkway

how silence consumes

the sound of rain through trees
feet hurriedly shuffling

night air

for all one knows

To masturbate a cosmos
top floor of a building
to decline a summer
weathered and lined, plated

to cut it down to the trunk
to exercise discretion

to go forward by steps, leaps
ankles

any other childhood

No man invisible
no man forgotten in himself
no transparent shadow

to walk a room
pliée
to walk

to decide
grocery cart

to have made a decision

To counter, parry
to act as ballast
to kiss the rings of foreign fingers

Venus the rival
wide open the spread

to question an account
traverse a distance

the drain the oil
permanent fixture

The red party and consequence
Oglethorpe's design

how the piedmonts are flush with forest
county fair calf

relocated crown and boat
symptoms of an empire

Christ the Christ and killed
message to his mother

four score and mule

That were lame
that were sparrow
that predicated the whole demise
stance
that said something Mr. Lusk could not hear
that trod well-trod walkways
that asked its weight in flesh
that said it understood
that said it said it said

A dutiful child
continent
the two mountains one must cross to leave

recondite
the Holy Ghost

all the things to suffer

how she selects her vegetables, eggs
her favorite vendors

how Tiamat was once free in the water

To divide a trust
to divide

the weight one carries
lonely bus

seraphim
mountain goats
well hidden geese

fettered
cavalcade

The one that came to visit
the one to take you out

contemplation of the rosary, penance
the need for final unction

how fables become canon
a body in state

how incense smells heroin-like
a hint of consideration

to learn from Lei

Mechanization and utility
to walk a short rope

hailed and bannered

what comes between

she selects shirts by material
overly wrought

fans through the market
Ionian

every wet lip

A lion's gait
a needle's eye

to get the camel to walk

to cross full fare
a shade all that is visible
coupled netting and squander

Mr. Lusk and a chain of events
Mr. Lusk quite mid-afternoon

Spring is nice where Spring is

To square the past
to determine a history
to study the levels of brick-lines
cinder blocks
to chart the cobble stones
use of pavement
planks along the boardwalk
to account for every shingle
nail used in antiquity

Settling of a foundation
movement

youth brigade and direction
how the wind changes line

what it's like near
Puebla Houston-Whitier

how it all racks up

how children talk between destinations
furthest from suffer

Every ante a bluff
social construct

down to the shit and dirt of things

an understanding of departure
confused moth
white-washed

academe

the books Mr. Lusk bought
the ones he intends to read

Utah in December
sandalwood
Ulysses

somehow we all fall
crenellated
mediaeval

saints and sandwiches
a good St. Chris
Aye. And more aye. Aye like you need it

The hem of her skirt
the hem

the decisions to be made

southward
departure

any other platform

field of cows

contingent

all the birds in Asia

How the heart pounds
pharosial
how the heart remains

how the trains run on time
picture perfect

regulated shipping channel
contrary current

how it all gets sorted
contingent

Shades without shadow
hope within

to tidy up the room
reposition a chair

to read too much
to think too little
to oversow a field

attribute of form
untenable grace

What Vladimir said
what he didn't
gunshot to the heart

what the newsreels ran that week
how they read decades later

how Mr. Lusk saw Bruce Lee films as a child
Civic Theatre

Lot's warning to forget the past
brine in the sea

The purpose of sketches
hagiography

that she wore red shoes
no longer seems to matter

a long lecture on decision
faculty of consequence

a short sweater season

listless Shelley and his brain

to reckon a human position

The conditions we are born in
the houses

historical society placard
monument to the dead
votives and progression

how they enter
how they exit
untrue to circumstance

how a bowl is too much to own

That Mr. Lusk liked her is not disputed
troubadour
how narrow the heart

that a Ferris wheel spins round
any state fair trope

fall what may fall

big stone building

how even the Earth shakes
at its own proportions

A dead collaboration
antipathy
all the tea in China

a sparrow confused
the sources

repentant
the walkway

reports from the field
okra in season

Hung high and well good
any other narrative

to feel the complications
to feel

one hill in one town is quite like another

a folding chair reunion
vaudeville
chorus girls

flag stuck on a heap of bones

How she worries

arson
an unplanned fire

to hold the bishop for opposition queen
to hold

matin chants
a bronze cast bell

Lincoln's failure
a deck of cards

To claim
to vent
Ariadne's loss

theodicy

mongoose and weasel
fall of an empire
ships returning to port

to cut one's hair
to change one's wardrobe

To do good
a saint's sepulcher
osiary

a history to attend to
a heritage

to walk in old man's shoes
to walk

the act of walking quite the same
well-beaten path

How Mr. Lusk would buy rounds
hopeless of recompense

to see everyone off at the station

how the rude forefathers of the hamlet slept

a question of accounting

to factor dog ears and marginalia
economy and nature
to posit a single voice

Simon among the sinners

Tapestry of a story
muted circumstance

Mr. Lusk in the park

the squirrel's granary is full
to be well prepared
regardless the scenery

noviate at the gate
compliance to the Rule

a set set of standards

How a crop dominates
how an arm is divided

the fallow section given rest
but only temporarily

to linger on a given topic
to linger
to consider the consequences
abuttals

to have one's doubts

The value of a name
byline

personified air and gendered
Hera

the two waves that fucked

sideshow poster
dutiful in its function

all the leisured women
depicted most leisurely

The purpose of any endeavor
shadowed valley
the gutter

how moods and tastes change
definition of Beauty

beatified but not sainted
Agobard

to have a disciple

Florus, a most minor poet

On this bridge and no other
the comings and goings of strangers

a body where thought would be
matrimonial compass

to come to a decision
cherry orchard

to decide

there is little way to rectify the past
all the well-read men, yes

This station for cleansing
cooking utensils

to roam the countryside unattended
beautiful blue Aryan eyes

to crush on every boy
to crush

to focus on a figure
aerospace

to ponder the distance

What Gagarin said
felt and thought
the consequence

Lewis' slow demise

what is not factored in
to factor

muled the attempt
like some branch of stars we see

a slow horse in a dead heat

Maupined
factoried
subtlety of shoes

to hold a crowd quiet
to hold one's own

the floorwalker and the escalator routine
the heist

Bodo and Herman the Jew

the extent of one's knowledge

How her purse coordinates
to get about the city
to weather the speeches

spirit or beam of an original
branded steer their field

tourniquet and sieve
to perform lesser miracles

where murmurs on
frog's eyed crow

To gut the bird and serve it
to gut

Cows of Bashan
the outline

failures and their precedents
feudal farm
finished cycle of ages

repetition of the factory floor
sound of steel-toed shoes

Book learnt and leisure
svelte women depicted
broodmare

Boethius
to calculate a demise
to navigate

oar against strong current
to speak a sign

the way one speaks

To one's own roof
Mars vacating
to a house of walls
interior

to collect, a calm
perhaps unfounded
to collect

to plan

—All right, but you have to promise not to cry

To near the finish
ostrich
the first snows of absence

to ratify beauty
to discard

to say nothing
else purse-lipped

a xerox of her passport photo
all reasonable requests

Even the Siren's sang
valescence
a calming

rocks and the shore
terrain

orange and green
a prayer shawl

wal-low
wander

ACKNOWLEDGEMENTS

I would like to thank the editors of the following journals, magazines and websites for publishing parts of this work: The Aerial Perspective, Backwards City Review, Boog City, Book of Matches, Cult of Clio, Denver Quarterly, Fire, First Offense, Five Fingers Review, Hudson Valley Writers Guild, Melbourne Culture Center, Merrymark, Noctua Review, Red Hawk Review, Tinfish, Traverse, and Zafusy.

The images and snippets of found material draw from varied sources such as Babylonian creation myths, Carolingian history, Marco Polo, Paul Éluard, Elizabeth Willis, Xinran, Seijun Suzuki's "Branded to Kill," and the Chase Park Girls.

DAVID HARRISON HORTON is a Beijing-based writer, artist, editor, and curator.

He's the author of the well-reviewed, genre-breaking Maze Poems (Arteidiola, 2022). His chapbooks include Model Answers (CCCP Chapbooks/Subpress, 2024), BeiHai (Nanjing Poetry, 2005), and Pete Hoffman Days (Pinball, 2003). His chapbook, Salt & Iron, was serialized by In Parentheses in 2020. His poetry has appeared in many respected publications, including The Oregon Review, Boog City, Denver Quarterly, The Belfast Review, Variant Literature, Roi Fainéant, Yolk, Verbal Art, and Pennsylvania English.

David has done poetry readings and performances across the United States, in Mexico, China, and Hong Kong. The venues include places like City Lights Books (San Francisco), Unnameable Books (New York), San Francisco State University, Picasso Machinery (New York), SUNY Buffalo, Hothouse (Chicago), Stanford University, University of Virginia, University of Las Vegas, Northwestern University (Chicago), Camera Stylo (Beijing), and Poetry Out Loud (Hong Kong), among others.

He has published and edited the poetry publications Chase Park (2000-2004), WORK (2008), and currently edits the Pushcart Award-winning SAGINAW (2011-present).

He currently curates the neo-benshi (movie-talking) nights for the Spittoon Collective in Beijing.

You can learn more about David at his website: davidharrisonhorton.com.

www.ingramcontent.com/pod-product-compliance
Lightning Source LLC
Chambersburg PA
CBHW060341080526
44584CB00013B/861